DOWNLOADS
FROM

BRENDA SUE RANDOLPH

Copyright © 2021 Brenda Sue Randolph.

All rights reserved. No part of this book may be used or reproduced by any means, graphic, electronic, or mechanical, including photocopying, recording, taping or by any information storage retrieval system without the written permission of the author except in the case of brief quotations embodied in critical articles and reviews.

This book is a work of non-fiction. Unless otherwise noted, the author and the publisher make no explicit guarantees as to the accuracy of the information contained in this book and in some cases, names of people and places have been altered to protect their privacy.

LifeRich Publishing is a registered trademark of The Reader's Digest Association, Inc.

LifeRich Publishing books may be ordered through booksellers or by contacting:

LifeRich Publishing
1663 Liberty Drive
Bloomington, IN 47403
www.liferichpublishing.com
844-686-9607

Because of the dynamic nature of the Internet, any web addresses or links contained in this book may have changed since publication and may no longer be valid. The views expressed in this work are solely those of the author and do not necessarily reflect the views of the publisher, and the publisher hereby disclaims any responsibility for them.

Any people depicted in stock imagery provided by Getty Images are models, and such images are being used for illustrative purposes only. Certain stock imagery © Getty Images.

Scripture taken from the New King James Version®. Copyright © 1982 by Thomas Nelson. Used by permission. All rights reserved.

ISBN: 978-1-4897-3335-1 (sc)
ISBN: 978-1-4897-3334-4 (hc)
ISBN: 978-1-4897-3336-8 (e)

Library of Congress Control Number: 2021903608

Print information available on the last page.

LifeRich Publishing rev. date: 02/19/2021

A GENTLE, QUIET SPIRIT

*T*HERE IS BEAUTY IN A gentle, quiet spirit, which is precious in My sight. The manner in which you live shows what is truly in your heart. A gentle, quiet spirit shows a calming love that is grounded in Me. A deep faith and trust shines forth from this type of person, whose happiness comes from pleasing Me and not from pleasing humankind.

> Rather *let it be* the hidden person of the heart, with the incorruptible *beauty* of a gentle and quiet spirit, which is very precious in the sight of God. (1 Peter 3:4)
>
> But as we have been approved by God to be entrusted with the gospel, even so we speak, not as pleasing men, but God who tests our hearts. (1 Thessalonians 2:4)

A TINY FLICKER

I AM THE LIGHT WHO SHINES through the darkest of nights. You are drawn to a tiny flicker of My light. There is a drawing power in this light. As you focus on the flicker, the light begins to get brighter, showing you the way to enter into My marvelous light. There you will find Me with open arms, ready to receive you into the light of my love, shining brightly on you.

> For it is the God who commanded light to shine out of darkness, who has shone in our hearts to *give* the light of the knowledge of the glory of God in the face of Jesus Christ. (2 Corinthians 4:6)
>
> Do not rejoice over me, my enemy; When I fall, I will arise; When I sit in darkness, The Lord *will* be a light to me. (Micah 7:8)

ALL THINGS ARE LAWFUL

*A*LL THINGS ARE LAWFUL FOR Me, but all things are not profitable. Think on and do things that are profitable for the kingdom of God. Many thoughts enter your mind for doing this or that, but is it profitable? You have many choices throughout the day; choose what will glorify your Father in heaven. Make wise choices and enjoy My blessings and favor in your life.

> All things are lawful for me, but not all things are helpful; all things are lawful for me, but not all things edify. (1 Corinthians 10:23)

> A wise *man* will hear and increase learning, And a man of understanding will attain wise counsel. (Proverbs 1:5)

BE CONTENT IN ME

*W*HEN YOU COVET WHAT SOMEONE else has, this is an act of idolatry. Any form of idolatry displeases Me. Keep your life free from the love of money, and be content with what you have. Contentment comes from an abiding relationship with Me. Happiness grows when you spend quality time with Me. You will not be searching for contentment elsewhere when you realize that I am all you need.

> Therefore put to death your members which are on the earth; fornication, uncleanness, passion, evil desire, and covetousness, which is idolatry. (Colossians 3:5)

> Let *your* conduct *be* without covetousness; be content with such things as you have. For He Himself has said, "I will never leave you nor forsake you." (Hebrews 13:5)

BE READY

*P*ICTURE ME COMING DOWN FROM heaven to rescue you from all trials and tribulations. Be ready for My return. Live in expectation that this could be the day. Live your life for what truly matters. Devote yourselves to prayer, keeping alert with an attitude of thanksgiving. Be ready, for I will come at an hour that you do not expect.

> Continue earnestly in prayer, being vigilant in it with thanksgiving. (Colossians 4:2)

> "But know this, that if the master of the house had known what hour the thief would come, he would have watched and not allowed his house to be broken into. Therefore you also be ready, for the Son of Man is coming at an hour you do not expect." (Luke 12:39–40)

BEAR ONE ANOTHER'S BURDENS

BEAR ONE ANOTHER'S BURDENS. THIS is the will of My Father. Lift up the concerns of those around you. Pray for your family and friends. Make time to show your love and concern for others. How you spend your time shows Me what is in your heart. When you serve your friends and family, you serve Me. These actions show My love for them through you.

> Bear one another's burdens, and so fulfill the law of Christ. (Galatians 6:2)

> But the Lord said to Samuel, "Do not look at his appearance or at his physical stature, because I have refused him. For *the Lord does* not *see* as man sees; for man looks at the outward appearance, but the Lord looks at the heart." (1 Samuel 16:7)

7

BEARING MUCH FRUIT

*Y*OU WILL DRAW STRENGTH FROM my unconditional love for you. I am the vine, and you are the branches. He who abides in Me, and I in him, bears much fruit, for without Me you can do nothing. I give you strength to do all things. Stay close to Me, and you will have all the strength you need. You will bear much fruit. My love will flow from Me to you and to others. This will produce fruit in your life that will glorify Me. Continue to abide in Me so your fruit will be plentiful.

> I am the vine, you *are* the branches. He who abides in Me, and I in him, bears much fruit; for without Me you can do nothing. (Matthew 15:5)

> I can do all things through Christ who strengthens Me. (Philippians 4:13)

BELIEVE IN ME

*C*AREFUL ANALYSIS OF MY WORD will give you an understanding of who I am. My love is reaching out to you, drawing you to the light of My presence. I want to receive you unto Myself and give you untold blessings. Receive My gift of salvation today and believe in Me. It would be a decision you would never regret.

> "And this is the will of Him who sent Me, that everyone who sees the Son and believes in Him may have everlasting life; and I will raise him up at the last day." (John 6:40)

> "For God so *loved* the world that He gave His only begotten Son, that whoever believes in Him should not perish but have everlasting life. (John 3:16)

BLESSED TO BE A BLESSING

My CHILDREN, I HAVE BLESSED you to be a blessing to others, giving of My love to be fast-forwarded to those around you. When I enrich you with blessings, My intentions are to see you share and bless others. Sharing your earthly treasures lays up treasures for you in heaven. For where your treasures are, your heart will be also.

> I will make you a great nation; I will bless you And make your name great; And you shall be a blessing. (Genesis 12:2)

> "Do not lay up for yourselves treasures on earth, where moth and rust destroy and where thieves break in and steal; but lay up for yourselves treasures in heaven, where neither moth nor rust destroys and where thieves do not break in and steal." (Matthew 6:19–20)

BRING ME YOUR PETITIONS

*E*XPECT POSITIVE RESULTS WHEN YOU bring your petitions to Me. Believe in faith that I am working on your behalf. Remember that My timing is perfect, and I will grant your petition when the time is right. Come to Me, desiring My perfect will above yours. I have the ability to see the beginning and ending of your situation. I will work all things together for good to those who love Me and are called according to My purpose.

> Be anxious for nothing, but in everything by prayer and supplication, with thanksgiving, let your requests be made known to God; (Philippians 4:6)
>
> And we know that all things work together for good to those who love God, to those who are the called according to *His* purpose. (Romans 8:28)

CALL OUT TO ME

*O*H, HOW MY HEART YEARNS for My people to trust Me to guide them. I am the way, the truth, and the life. Things would be so much easier if you would come to Me first, before you begin your day. I am waiting with open arms to bless your day, if only you would ask for My help and direction. My heart longs to hear your voice calling out to Me. My Spirit leaps with joy when I hear you call out.

> Jesus said to him, "I am the way, the truth, and the life. No one comes to the Father except through Me. (John 14:6)

> Call to Me, and I will answer you, and show you great and mighty things, which you do not know. (Jeremiah 33:3)

CHRISTLIKE QUALITIES

Qualities that show you have My Spirit within you are love, joy, peace, patience, kindness, goodness, faithfulness, gentleness, and self-control. Many others come to mind, such as humility, forgiveness, honesty, encouragement, and generosity. Your life should demonstrate to others these qualities. It is possible to show these qualities in your life when you trust Me with all your heart to lead you daily. Let My Holy Spirit guide you with all wisdom. You will grow in your relationship with Me as you live out these principles in your life.

> But the fruit of the Spirit is love, joy, peace, longsuffering, *kindness*, goodness, faithfulness, gentleness, self-control. Against such there is no law. (Galatians 5:22–23)
>
> For to one is given the word of wisdom through the Spirit, to another the word of knowledge through the same Spirit. (1 Corinthians 12:8)

COMFORT THE MOURNING

I WILL COMFORT THE MOURNING. I give peace to those who mourn. I am aware of the deep pain and loss you feel. My arms are around you, holding you up through this time of excruciating loss. Know that My love engulfs your spirit as you suffer loss. Separation from a loved one is extremely painful. This gives you a glimpse of what the pain of living separately from your heavenly Father would be like—an emptiness of a greater degree. Be ever thankful for your relationship with your Father through Jesus, the Son.

> Blessed are those who mourn, for they shall be comforted. (Matthew 5:4)

> Fear not for I *am* with you; Be not dismayed, for I *am* your God. I will strengthen you, Yes, I will help you, I will uphold you with My righteous right hand. (Isaiah 41:10)

CONFLICTS AROUND YOU

*D*O NOT LOOK AROUND YOU at the many conflicts that are presently piercing your thoughts. They are all momentary events that tend to pull your thoughts away from Me. Anxious thoughts will cause panic and fear to engulf your mind. Immediately recognize that this is the enemy who desires only to steal, kill, and destroy. Turn your thoughts back to Me, the one who comforts and delights your soul.

> The thief does not come except to steal, kill, and to destroy. I have come that they may have life, and that they may have it more *abundantly*. (John 10:10)

> In the multitude of my anxieties within me, Your comforts delight my soul. (Psalm 94:19)

15

DO NOT DOUBT

*W*HEN YOU COME TO ME with your petitions, ask in faith with no doubting. If you doubt I will hear or answer your prayers, you are like a wave of the sea driven and tossed by the wind. You cannot expect to receive anything from Me when you are double-minded and unstable in all your ways. Ask Me for the faith to believe without any doubting, and the things you ask for you will receive.

> But let him ask in faith, with no doubting, for he who doubts is like a wave of the sea driven and tossed by the wind. For let not that man suppose that he will receive anything from the Lord; *he is* a double-minded man, unstable in all his ways. (James 1:6–8)
>
> "Therefore I say to you whatever things you ask when you pray, believe that you receive *them*, and you will have *them*." (Mark 11:24)

DO NOT ENVY

*D*O NOT LET ENVY OR jealously steal your joy. Do not look to what others possess and covet what they have. Be at peace with the life I have given you. Satan uses this visual tactic to draw you into a place of dissatisfaction. Recognize who the enemy is and turn your thoughts back to Me and what I am doing. Be thankful for the blessings that you have. Keep your mind focused on the true prize, knowing you are receiving a kingdom that cannot be shaken.

> For where envy and self-seeking *exist*, confusion and every evil thing *are* there. (James 3:16)

> Therefore, since we are receiving a kingdom which cannot be shaken, let us have grace, by which we may serve God acceptably with reverence and godly fear. (Hebrews 12:28)

EMPOWERED BY THE HOLY SPIRIT

$\mathcal{W}$HEN YOU ACCEPT ME AS Lord and Savior, I empower you with the Holy Spirit. He enables you to accomplish all that is needed in your life. Remember you have the Holy Spirit living within you, which allows you to do all things through Christ who gives you strength. When trials come, the Holy Spirit gives you power to overcome them. You have the strength needed to live above your circumstances. What a beautiful gift!

> I can do all things through Christ who strengthens me. (Philippians 4:13)

> Then Peter said to them, Repent, and let every one of you be baptized in the name of Jesus Christ for the remission of sins; and you shall receive the gift of the Holy Spirit. (Acts 2:38)

ENJOY FOREVERMORE

*K*EEP WALKING ON THE NARROW path, for wide is the road that leads to destruction. There are many turns in the road that try to lead you off course. Stay focused on Me and the narrow path that leads you to peace and a life full of joy. Seek Me daily, so you will not make a wrong turn. I can help you stay on the path that will lead you into My everlasting arms—a place of overpowering love and joy unspeakable, designed for you to enjoy forevermore.

> "Enter by the narrow gate; for wide is the gate and broad is the way that leads to destruction, and there are many who go in by it. Because narrow is the gate and difficult is the way which leads to life, and there are few who find it." (Matthew 7:13–14)
>
> And you will seek Me and find *Me*, when you search for Me with all your heart. (Jeremiah 29:13)

FEAR IS IN THE MIND

$\mathcal{B}$REAK APART ANY STRONGHOLD OF fear upon you. Enter My rest. I will lift the fear off of you and bring you into a place of peace and rest. The battle to break apart fear is in the mind. Let My words give you all that you need to fight the battle. Fear not, for I am with you. Be comforted in knowing that you are not alone. Accepting Me as Lord gives you the power to live above fear in your life.

> For God has not given us the spirit of fear, but of power and of love and of a *sound mind*. (2 Timothy 1:7)

> "Have I not commanded you? *Be strong* and of good courage; do not be afraid, nor be dismayed, for the Lord your God *is* with you wherever you go." (Joshua 1:9)

20

FEED YOUR SPIRIT

I TAKE CARE OF THE BIRDS of the air, and I will take care of you. Feed your spirit, for it is more important to nurture the spirit than the physical body. The Word is all empowering to feed your spirit. It will strengthen you to live a strong spiritual life. Feast on it daily for what you need to grow in Me. You will be filled and satisfied when you feast on My Word.

> "Look at the birds of the air, for they neither sow nor reap nor gather into barns; yet your heavenly Father feeds them. Are you not of more value than they?" (Matthew 6:26)

> Blessed *are* those who hunger and thirst for righteousness, For they shall be filled. (Matthew 5:6)

FELLOWSHIP WITH ME

LIVING CLOSE TO ME IS a form of worship. It shows Me where your heart is in our relationship. This was My plan from the beginning of creation, enjoying fellowship together every day, walking and talking together in the beautiful garden I created for you. Eve was tempted by the serpent and disobeyed. Her choice, along with Adam, caused death to become a reality. My desire has been to bring you back into perfect communion with Me. I was crucified on a rugged cross to make My perfect plan possible for you once again.

> Sing to the Lord! Praise the Lord! For He has delivered the life of the poor From the hand of evildoers. (Jeremiah 20:13)
>
> And they heard the sound of Lord God walking in the garden in the cool of the day, and Adam and his wife hid themselves from the presence of the Lord God among the trees of the garden. (Genesis 3:8)

FOLLOW MY COUNSEL

*T*HERE ARE MANY PLANS WITHIN the hearts of My people. Encourage them to listen to My counsel. Those who listen to me show their love and devotion to Me. I will increase the understanding of those who purpose in their hearts to follow My counsel. You will succeed in life when you listen to Me. My blessings will be poured out on you.

> There are many plans in a man's heart, Nevertheless the Lord's counsel—that will stand. (Proverbs 19:21)

> A wise *man* will hear and increase learning, And a man of understanding will attain wise counsel. (Proverbs 1:5)

FORGIVE TO BE FORGIVEN

*Y*OU MUST FORGIVE OTHERS SO that you may be forgiven. Your heart must be clear of any unforgiveness so that your prayers will not be hindered. Unforgiveness is a sin that will keep you from walking close to Me. Seek Me to help you practice forgiveness when the need arises. I have the power to break the hold of unforgiveness on you.

> "And whenever you stand praying, if you have anything against anyone, forgive him, that your Father in heaven may also forgive you your trespasses. But if you do not forgive, neither will your Father in heaven forgive your trespasses." (Mark 11:25–26)
>
> And be kind to one another, tenderhearted, forgiving one another, even as God in Christ forgave you. (Ephesians 4:32)

GIVE ME THIS DAY

I AM GUARDING YOUR THOUGHTS AND keeping watch over the door of your lips. I am your protector and defender. Give Me this day so that blessings I have prepared for you will be experienced. I delight in giving good gifts to My children. You are precious in My sight. Release your will and plan into My hands so that your joy may be full. I am the only one who knows what will bring overflowing joy into your life. Trust Me to give you that joy-filled life you long for.

> Set a guard, O Lord, over my mouth; Keep watch over the door of my lips. (Psalm 141:3)

> "If you then, being evil, know how to give good gifts to your children, how much more will your Father who is in heaven give good things to those who ask Him!" (Matthew 7:11)

GIVE ME YOUR CARES

*B*E NOT DISMAYED, FOR I am with you wherever you go. Listen carefully for My voice. I am there, even in the midst of chaos. Move your mind past the chaos of this world and center your mind on Me. I am the author and finisher of your faith. Lift your voice to Me, and I will hear your cries even before you speak a word. I hear your heart's desire and am aware of your thoughts. Trust Me to guide you down the path of life.

> Casting all your care upon Him, for He cares for you. (1 Peter 5:7)

> Delight yourself also in the Lord, And He shall give you the desires of your heart. (Psalm 37:4)

GLORIFIED THROUGH SUFFERING

I CAN BE GLORIFIED THROUGH YOU in the manner in which you suffer. Your demeanor and actions through your suffering can show others your faith and love for Me. Suffering comes to all in this journey of life. How you persevere through these times of suffering shows volumes about your character and your relationship with Me. Always ask for My wisdom and power to get through times of suffering with grace.

> Yet if *anyone suffers* as a Christian, let him not be ashamed, but let him glorify God in this matter. (1 Peter 4:16)

> And not only *that,* but we also glory in tribulations, knowing that tribulation produces perseverance, character; and character, hope. (Romans 5:3–4)

I AM THE GIFT GIVER

*B*RING ME YOUR TITHES AND offerings. You cannot outgive Me. I am the giver of precious gifts—gifts that you truly need, gifts that do not disappoint. My presence in your life is a gift. Embrace My gifts. Breathe in the fresh air of My presence. Enjoy the peaceful calm of the flowing river of My love. Be comforted by the gentle breeze of My Spirit flowing through you. Use the gift of My love to bless those around you.

> "Bring all the tithes into the storehouse, That there may be food in My house, And try Me now in this," Says the Lord of hosts, "If I will not open for you the windows of heaven And pour out for you *such* blessing That *there will* not *be* room enough *to receive it.*" (Malachi 3:10)

> The Spirit of God has made me, And the breath of the Almighty gives me life. (Job 33:4)

I AM THE POTTER

*B*LESS THE LORD O MY soul and all that is within me. Praise His holy name. For I am the Potter, and you are the clay. Allow Me to mold and make you after My will. Pour out your heart to Me, and I will listen. Open the door that I have placed before you. Walk through in blind trust that I will guide you every step of the way. I will strengthen you for the task ahead.

> Bless the Lord, O my soul; And all that is within me, *bless* His holy name! (Psalm 103:1)

> But now, O Lord, You *are* our Father; We *are* the clay, and You our potter; And all we *are* the work of Your hand. (Isaiah 64:8)

I AM YOUR JOY

$\mathcal{S}$URRENDERING YOUR WILL TO ME allows Me to give you wisdom and spiritual understanding, for I know your thoughts before you speak them. Clear your thoughts so I can speak to you. Believe Me and trust Me with your life. I will bless you with a joyful heart that can rest peacefully. I am your joy. Do not look elsewhere for it. I am the only one who can satisfy the longing of your soul.

> For this reason we also, since the day we heard it, do not cease to pray for you, and to ask that you may be filled with knowledge of His will in all wisdom and spiritual understanding. (Colossians 1:9)

> "For I *know* their works and their thoughts, It shall be that I will gather all nations and tongues; and they shall come and see My glory." (Isaiah 66:18)

I AM YOUR SOURCE

I AM YOUR SOURCE FOR ALL things truly profitable in this life. Material things acquired in this life do not bring satisfaction. It is a very short-lived joy, fleeting very quickly. When you tap into My source of living a Christ-centered life, joy and peace flood your mind. There is a deep satisfaction that penetrates your being. A love of serving others will become the drive that motivates you. This is what a successful life in My eyes looks like.

> You will show me the path of life; In Your presence is fullness of joy; At Your right hand *are* pleasures forevermore. (Psalm 16:11)
>
> *Serve* the Lord with gladness; Come before His presence with singing. (Psalm 100:2)

31

I HEAR YOUR CRIES

I HEAR YOUR CRIES COMING UP before Me. I stand ready to comfort you and guide you. Ask and you shall receive. Seek and you shall find Me ready to help you in times of need. Do not be afraid to ask Me for your needs. You are precious to Me. I hold your next breath in My hand. Great is My faithfulness to you. You can trust that I will never leave you or forsake you. I am your Father and your God.

> *Ask*, and it will be given to you; seek, and you will find; knock, and it will be opened to you. (Matthew 7:7)

> "Be strong and of good courage, do not fear nor be afraid of them; for the Lord your God, He *is* the One who goes with you. He will not leave you nor forsake you." (Deuteronomy 31:6)

UNDERSTAND YOUR THOUGHTS

My EYES SAW YOUR SUBSTANCE before you were formed. This truth is an unfathomable fact. The mind cannot comprehend it all. I am acquainted with all of your ways. I understand your thoughts from afar. I am intricately entwined with the thoughts of My children. They listen to My voice, and I know them.

> Your eyes saw my substance, being yet unformed. And in Your book they all were written, The days fashioned for me, When *as yet there were* none of them. (Psalm 139:16)

> "My sheep hear My voice, and I know them, and they follow Me." (John 10:27)

33

I WILL DIRECT YOUR STEPS

*T*HERE WILL BE PEACE IN the midst of the storm for those who know Me, who truly know Me—those who want My plan and will for their lives, those who give all of themselves to Me. My children who walk humbly beside Me daily, choosing to follow My leading. You may plan your way forward, but I will direct your steps. Whoever trusts in Me is happy deep down in the recesses of their heart and mind.

> When you pass through the *waters*, I *will be* with you; And through the rivers they shall not overflow you. When you walk through the fire, you shall not be burned, Nor shall the flame scorch you. (Isaiah 43:2)
>
> A man's heart plans his way, But the Lord directs his steps. (Proverbs 16:9)

IN THE QUIETNESS OF THE MORNING

*W*AIT PATIENTLY FOR ME TO speak to you in the quietness of the morning. Empty your thoughts that I might enter them and feed you wisdom. Listen for My still, small voice. I want to renew your mind for the day ahead. Give Me your cares and rest in Me. This will help you enjoy what I have prepared for you. I am able to do exceedingly and abundantly above all that you ask or think. Stand resolute in the quietness of My very presence.

> And do not be *conformed* to this world, but be transformed by the renewing of your mind, that you may prove what *is* that good and acceptable and perfect will of God. (Romans 12:2)
>
> Now to Him who is able to do exceedingly abundantly above all that we ask or think, according to the power that works in us. (Ephesians 3:20)

35

INDESCRIBABLE BLESSINGS

I HAVE INDESCRIBABLE BLESSINGS AWAITING FOR those who love Me. My plan for you is so much better than yours. Ask Me to show you My plan daily. You will grow in your love for Me as you follow and listen to My still, small voice whispering to you. It blesses Me when you listen and follow along the path I am showing you. Your faithfulness will bring great satisfaction and comfort to your soul.

> But as it is written: "Eye has not seen, nor ear heard, Nor have entered into the heart of man The things which God has prepared for those who love Him."
> (1 Corinthians 2:9)

> And after the earthquake a fire, but the Lord was not in the fire; and after the fire a still small voice.
> (1 Kings 19:12)

LET ME DIRECT YOUR PATH

$\mathcal{I}$ AM WORKING ON YOUR BEHALF. I am listening to your thoughts. I know all you are thinking before you say a word. Let me direct your path today, fulfilling the plan I have for you. Peace and joy I give to you now and forever. Rest in My promises. Let your love light shine forth. There is much to accomplish today. I will lead you and guide you.

> The Lord knows the thoughts of man, that they *are* futile. (Psalm 94:11)

> And do not be *conformed* to this world, but be transformed by the renewing of your mind, that you may prove what is that good and acceptable and perfect will of God. (Romans 12:2)

37

LET ME HAVE YOUR WORRIES

KEEP YOUR EYES FOCUSED ON Me. I will give you what you need for today. I will strengthen you for the task ahead. Bend your will to Me. Let Me have your worries. I will carry your load. Peace and joy will be yours when you give Me the problems that are pressing you down. I will lift the burden off you. I am here for you. Trust Me to give you all that you need for a successful and fruitful day.

> Cast your burden on the Lord, And He shall *sustain* you; He shall never permit the righteous to be moved. (Psalm 55:22)

> I WILL love You, O Lord, my strength. The Lord is my rock and my fortress and my deliverer; My God, my strength, in whom I will trust; My shield and the horn of my salvation, my stronghold. (Psalm 18:1–2)

LET ME HELP YOU

NOTHING GOING ON IN THE world is a surprise to Me. I am omnipotent (all-knowing). I want to help you navigate through this life. You must come to Me continually throughout the day. I am ready to assist you at all times. Life can be very difficult, especially when you do not ask for My help. Let Me help you, my child, to flow more easily through your days. Nothing is impossible with Me guiding you along the way.

> And I heard, as it were, the voice of a great multitude, as the sound of many waters and as the sound of mighty thunderings, saying, "Alleluia! For the Lord God Omnipotent reigns!" (Revelation 19:6)

> "For with God nothing will be impossible."
> (Luke 1:37)

39

LET YOUR THOUGHTS BE PURE

LET YOUR THOUGHTS BE PURE and without reproach. Choose to remove any negative or destructive thoughts that come into your mind. Be alert in knowing where these unfruitful, negative thoughts are coming from. When they enter your mind, immediately rebuke Satan in the name of Jesus. This will allow you to continue to receive My direction and truth for you, unhindered.

> Finally, brethren, whatever things are true, whatever things *are* noble, whatever things *are* just, whatever things *are* pure, whatever things *are* lovely, whatever things *are* of *good report*, if *there is* any virtue and if *there is* anything praiseworthy—meditate on these things. (Philippians 4:8)
>
> Casting down arguments and every high thing that exalts itself against the knowledge of God, bringing every thought into captivity to the *obedience* of Christ. (2 Corinthians 10:5)

40

LIFE PASSES QUICKLY

Realize that every minute of every day is a precious gift. I am the giver of all good things. I am watching over you at all times, for I never slumber or sleep. You are precious in My sight. Life passes by quickly; it is but a vapor that appears for a little time, then vanishes away. Use the minutes you have to leave a legacy of giving yourself to the needs of those around you. These actions will profit you now and in the life to come.

> Behold, He who keeps Israel Shall neither slumber nor sleep. (Psalm 121:4)

> Whereas you do not know what *will happen* tomorrow. For what is your life? It is even a vapor that appears for a little time and then vanishes away. (James 4:14)

41

LISTEN TO MY VOICE

WHEN YOU AWAKE IN THE morning, I am with you. I watch you sleep and walk beside you throughout the day. I am your constant companion. Life is but a vapor. It appears for a little time and then vanishes away. Use your precious time wisely. There is so much to accomplish. Listen to My voice and follow My leading. You will have the peace of God that surpasses all understanding. Life-changing accomplishments will get done when you choose to listen to Me and follow My direction.

> Whereas you do not know what *will happen* tomorrow. For what *is* your life? It is even a vapor that appears for a little time and then vanishes away. (James 4:14)

> And the peace of God, which surpasses all understanding, will guard your hearts and minds through Christ Jesus. (Philippians 4:7)

LONGINGS OF YOUR HEART

*S*PEAK TO ME ABOUT THE longings of your heart. I already know your thoughts but want to have this conversation with you. Tell Me about your deep longings that you guard yourself from thinking about. Bring them to the throne of grace and lay them at My feet. Together we will bring them into the light to reveal truth to you. I will help you move forward with the longings and desires I have planted within you. All things work together for good for those who love Me and are called according to My purpose.

> "Oh, that I might have my request, That God would grant *me* the thing that I long for!" (Job 6:8)

> And we know that all things work together for good to those who love God, to those who are called according to *His* purpose. (Romans 8:28)

43

LOVE CHANGES THE WORLD

LOVE IS THE GREATEST GIFT ever given. Love changes the world for good. Without love, all other gifts are meaningless. Love never fails. Stir up the gift of love within you and watch the results of love change the world. Love is irresistible to those who come into contact with it. It is a powerful gift that shines brightly in a dark world.

> And though I have *the gift* of prophecy, and understand all mysteries and all knowledge, and though I have all faith, so that I could remove mountains, but have not love, I am nothing. (1 Corinthians 13:2)

> Love never fails. But whether *there are* prophecies, they will fail; whether *there are* tongues, they will cease; whether *there is* knowledge, it will vanish away. (1 Corinthians 13:8)

44

LOVE IS POWERFUL

LOVE IS POWERFUL AND ABLE to change the hearts of evil men. Love came down from heaven and completely changed the world. I sacrificed it all to save you from the curse of fallen man. Without Me, there would be no hope. The abundant life would not be possible. So, take heart; I have overcome the world. Accept My sacrifice, the atonement for your sins. You can have the abundant life with peace and joy.

> "For God so *loved* the world that He gave His only begotten Son, that whoever believes in Him should not perish but have everlasting life." (John 3:16)

> "These things I have spoken to you, that in Me you may have peace. In the world you will have *tribulation*; but be of good cheer, I have overcome the world." (John 16:33)

45

LOVE LIGHT

My LOVE IS ABOUT GIVING to others to help them see Me more clearly. I want My children to be closely connected to Me. I want them to feel how much I love them. When you draw close to Me, My love light will shine brightly through you to others. Others will be drawn to this light in you. When I see you shining My light, it makes Me smile.

> Then Jesus spoke to them again, saying, "I am the light of the world. He who follows Me shall not walk in darkness, but have the light of life." (John 8:12)

> "Let your light so shine before men, that they may see your good works and glorify your Father in heaven." (Matthew 5:16)

46

LOVE YOUR NEIGHBOR

LOVE YOUR NEIGHBOR AS YOURSELF; in doing so, you show that you love Me. Follow the pattern of loving others as I have set before you. Your joy will be so overflowing that it cannot be contained. This is a command and not a suggestion. I know what will bring unspeakable joy to My children. Trust and follow Me in the way I lead you to go.

> "'And you shall love the Lord your God with all your heart, with all your soul, with all your *mind*, and with all your strength.' This is the first commandment. And the second, like it, is this: 'You shall love your neighbor as yourself.' There is no other commandments greater than these." (Mark 12:30–31)
>
> And may the Lord make you increase and abound in love to one another and to all, just as we do to you. (1 Thessalonians 3:12)

47

MY AVAILABLE POWER

WHO AM I THAT EVEN the winds and sea obey Me? My Spirit hovers over the entire universe and shows you My truth. I give power to the weak and strength to the powerless. Your mind is not able to comprehend the extent of My power. Accept by faith these truths and enjoy My blessings that help you live above your circumstances. My power is available to My children when they ask for it.

> So the men marveled, saying, "Who can this be, that even the winds and sea obey Him?" (Matthew 8:27)

> And my speech and my preaching *were* not with persuasive words of human wisdom but in demonstration of the Spirit and of power, that your faith should not be in the wisdom of men but in the power of God. (1 Corinthians 2:4–5)

48

MY FACE SHINES UPON YOU

AS MY FACE SHINES UPON you, I smile at the person you are becoming. You are being molded into My image. You seek My face in the morning and my direction throughout the day. My blessings are falling on you even when you seem unaware of them. The glow within you is getting much brighter as you draw closer to Me.

> The Lord make His face shine upon you, And be gracious to you. (Numbers 6:25)

> But we all, with unveiled face, beholding as in a mirror the glory of the Lord, are being transformed into the same image from glory to glory, just as the Spirit of the Lord. (2 Corinthians 3:18)

49

MY LOVE FOR YOU

How GREAT IS MY LOVE for you? Greater than the stars in the sky and the sand on the seashore. It is far and wide and cannot be measured. It expands the universe. My love unites all human existence. My love is unfailing. You can entrust your very life to Me. Whoever does not love does not know God, for God is love. My love endures forever.

> Cause Me to hear Your lovingkindness in the morning, For in You do I trust; Cause me to know the way in which I should walk, For I lift up my soul to You. (Psalm 143:8)
>
> He who does not love does not know God, for God is love. (1 John 4:8)

MY PLAN IS TO BLESS YOU

*Y*OU SHALL STILL BEAR FRUIT in old age. You still have a purpose here, as long as you live. I continue to be with you, showing you My will and My way. Only you can fulfill the plan I intentionally have for your life. Each of My children are special and unique. You have various gifts I have given you to fulfill the plan for your life. My plan is to bless you and be with you through this journey called life.

> They shall bear fruit in old age; They shall be fresh and flourishing. (Psalm 92:14)

> As each one has received a gift, minister it to one another, as good *stewards* of the manifold grace of God. (1 Peter 4:10)

51

MY PRESENCE

$\mathcal{S}$TARTING YOUR DAY OFF IN My presence gives you a safety net for the day. Team up with Me for a successful day. A calming sense of My presence will help you react in a Christlike manner. Give Me praise for what I am doing in your life. There are amazing benefits in teaming up with the lover of your soul.

> You will show me the path of life; In Your presence *is* fullness of joy; At your right hand *are* pleasures forevermore. (Psalm 16:11)

> For all that is in the world—the lust of the flesh, the lust of the eyes, and the pride of life—is not of the Father but is of the world. And the world is passing away, and the lust of it; but he who does the will of God abides forever. (1 John 2:16–17)

52

MY TRUTHS

I SPEAK FROM THE DEPTHS OF My heart the truths I have imparted to you: Those who seek Me shall not lack any good thing. I will hear your cries and deliver you out of your many afflictions. I will be faithful to you and show you My loving kindness. When you delight in Me, I will give you the desires of your heart.

> The young lions lack and suffer hunger; but those who seek the Lord shall not lack any good *thing*. (Psalm 34:10)

> Delight yourself also in the Lord, And He shall give you the desires of your *heart*. (Psalm 37:4)

53

MY WILL BE DONE

I DESIRE THAT MY WILL BE done on earth as it is in heaven. I desire your cooperation in getting My will to be done on earth. Your life runs smoother when you desire My will over yours. Commit your works to Me, and your thoughts will be established. Wisdom will be imparted to you, and knowledge and understanding will guide your way forward. He who has knowledge spares his words, and a man of understanding is of a calm spirit.

> *Commit* your works to the Lord, And your thoughts will be established. (Proverbs 16:3)

> He who has knowledge spares his words, *And* a man of understanding is of a calm spirit. (Proverbs 17:27)

54

MY WILL FOR YOU

*F*OCUS ON MY WILL FOR your life. Let go of trying to control situations in your life. You think you know what will make you happy, but do you? Examine this question with the determination to find truth. Put your faith and trust in Me, who holds your next breath in My hands. I am acquainted with all of your ways. There is nothing hidden from Me.

> "And you have lifted yourself up against the Lord of heaven. They have brought the vessels of His house before you, and you and your lords, your wives and your concubines, have drunk wine from them. And you have praised the gods of silver and gold, bronze and iron, wood and stone, which do not hear or see or know; and the God who *holds* your breath in His hand, and owns all your ways, you have not glorified." (Daniel 5:23)

> You comprehend my path and my lying down, And are acquainted with all my ways. (Psalm 139:3)

55

OVERCOME SATANIC ATTACKS

*S*PEND TIME WITH ME IN the quietness of the early morning. I will give you all you need to tackle the happenings of your day. Together we will overcome satanic attacks. Love will overcome the fiery darts coming at you. I am the solid rock on which you stand. I will not be moved. Saturate your heart and mind with the Word of God. It will give you ammunition for the battles that come. Remember that calling on My name will give you power to move mountains. With Me, you have the ability to overcome any trial.

> To declare that the Lord is upright; *He is* my rock, and *there is* no unrighteousness in Him. (Psalm 92:15)

> He shall call upon Me, and I will answer him; I *will be* with him in trouble; I will deliver him and honor him. (Psalm 91:15)

PEACE IN JESUS

PEACE BE STILL. MY PEACE I give to you, not as the world gives. I am with you and in you. Though there is chaos around you, there is peace within you. Focus on the peace, not the chaos. Live the plan I have for you, a plan to prosper you and not to harm you. Ask for My wisdom daily. I want to give you hope and a future. Life is from everlasting to everlasting. Peace be still.

> "Peace I leave with you, My peace I give to you; not as the world gives do I give to you. Let not your heart be troubled, neither let it be afraid." (John 14:27)

> For I know the thoughts that I think toward you, says the Lord, thoughts of peace and not of evil, to give you a future and a hope. (Jeremiah 29:11)

57

PEACE WILL FALL ON YOU

I WILL WALK WITH YOU IN the cool of the evening, reflecting on our productive day. Together there is nothing that will be impossible for us to accomplish. I give power to the weak and strength to the weary. When you trust Me, I give you all that is needed to accomplish the tasks ahead of you. Mercy and grace will be gifted to you in time of need. Peace will fall on you and guard your mind. Keep Me ever in the forefront of your mind. It will keep you in perfect peace. My love for you is unending. It is a perfect love that endures forever.

> He gives power to the weak, and to those who have no might He increases strength. (Isaiah 40:29)

> Let us therefore come boldly to the throne of grace, that we may obtain mercy and find grace to help in time of need. (Hebrews 4:16)

58

PRAYING IN MY WILL

*F*AITH IS KEY IN RECEIVING answers to your prayers. I have given good instruction in My Word for how I want you to pray. Pray that you do not enter into temptation. Pray for your enemies, your government leaders, missionaries, and those who preach the Gospel. Also pray for healing, salvation, forgiveness, wisdom, and boldness to speak My truths in love. These are some ways you can pray according to My will.

> "Watch and pray, lest you enter into temptation. The spirit indeed is willing, but the flesh is weak." (Matthew 26:41)

> Now this is the confidence that we have in Him, that if we ask anything according to His will, He hears us. And if we know that He hears us, whatever we ask we know that we have the petitions that we have asked of Him. (1 John 5:14–15)

PREPARATION IS KEY

I WILL BREAK OPEN THE WINDOWS of heaven and pour out My blessings on you. Keep your eyes and ears attentive to what I am doing around you. Open your heart to new beginnings. Life is a journey of hills and valleys. Preparation is key to living a joy-filled life. Stay in My Word to prepare you for the valleys of life. I will even make a way in the wilderness and rivers in the desert.

> "This book of the law shall not depart from your mouth, but you shall meditate in it day and night, that you may observe to do according to all that is written in it. For then you will make your way prosperous, and then you will have good success." (Joshua 1:8)

> Behold, I will do a new thing, Now it shall spring forth; Shall you not know it? I will even make a road in the wilderness *And* rivers in the desert. (Isaiah 43:19)

PUT ON YOUR ARMOR

IT IS BENEFICIAL FOR YOU to put on the whole armor of God, so that you may stand against the cunning ways of the devil. Take the shield of faith so that you may be able to quench the fiery darts coming at you. Stand in truth, wearing the breastplate of righteousness. Take the helmet of salvation and the sword of the Spirit, which is the Word of God. This prepares you to fight the good fight.

> Put on the whole armor of God, that you may be able to stand against the wiles of the devil. (Ephesians 6:11)

> Stand therefore, having girded your waist with truth, having put on the breastplate of righteousness, and having shod your feet with the preparation of the gospel of peace. (Ephesians 6:14–15)

61

RECEIVE MY LOVE

I HAVE INSCRIBED YOU ON THE palms of My hands. I will not forget you. You are in My thoughts continually. You can trust Me, who formed you from the womb. My love is steadfast and endures forever. Accept and receive My love for you. I am patiently waiting for you to respond to Me. I was sent to be the propitiation for your sins.

> See, I have inscribed you on the palms of *My hands*; Your walls are continually before Me. (Isaiah 49:16)

> In this the love of God was manifested toward us, that God has sent His only begotten Son into the world, that we might live through Him. In this is love, not that we loved God, but that He loved us and sent His Son *to be* the *propitiation* for our sins. (1 John 4:9–10)

REFLECTING ON OUR DAY

I WILL WALK WITH YOU IN the cool of the evening, reflecting on our productive day. Together there is nothing that is impossible for us to accomplish. I give power to the weak and strength to the weary. When you trust Me, I give you all that is needed to accomplish the tasks ahead of you. Mercy and grace will be gifted to you in time of need. Peace will fall on you and guard your mind. Keep Me ever in the forefront of your mind. It will keep you in perfect peace.

> He gives power to the weak, And to *those who have no might He increases strength.* (Isaiah 40:29)
>
> Let us therefore come boldly to the throne of grace, that we may obtain mercy and find grace to help in time of need. (Hebrews 4:16)

63

RELEASE ANGER

*B*RING ME YOUR THOUGHTS OF anger, and I will dispel them. Release the troubling thoughts to Me, and do not try to hold onto them. I will replace these thoughts with an all-encompassing peace. Your countenance and demeanor will relax as you encounter the overwhelming sense of peace that I will give you. The gift of peace transforms your thoughts and allows your mind and body to achieve the goal of complete relaxation.

> Cease from anger, and forsake wrath; Do not fret— it only *causes* harm. (Psalm 37:8)

> And let the peace of God rule in your hearts, to which also you were called in one body; and be thankful. (Colossians 3:15)

64

SEEDS OF MY LOVE

*W*E ARE WORKING TOGETHER TO bring about a harvest. Seeds of My love are planted, and another comes along and waters this fertile ground. The seed begins to grow into a beautiful plant that expands its fruit and reaches upward. My love is helping the plant blossom and grow into beautiful, mature fruit to be harvested.

> We then, as workers together *with Him* also plead with *you* not to receive the grace of God in vain. (2 Corinthians 6:1)

> I planted, Apollos watered, but God gave the increase. So then neither he who plants is anything, nor he who waters, but God who gives the increase. (1 Corinthians 3:6–7)

BRENDA SUE RANDOLPH

SEEK ME EARLY AND ALL DAY LONG

SEEK MY FACE EARLY IN the morning. Lift up your voice to Me. Give Me your attention. I want to have a conversation with you. It keeps our relationship fresh and anew. I care about the smallest details of your life. Include Me in all of your decisions throughout the day. I want to help you achieve the abundant life. Joy and peace are included in that. Rest in My everlasting arms.

> Trust in the Lord with all your heart, And lean not on your own understanding; In all your ways acknowledge Him, And He shall direct your paths. (Proverbs 3:5–6)

> "The thief does not come except to steal, and to kill, and to destroy. I have come that they may have life, and that they may have it more abundantly." (John 10:10)

SET YOUR LOVE UPON ME

*W*HEN YOU SET YOUR LOVE upon Me, I will answer you when you call out to Me. I will be with you when trouble comes. You will have My love to strengthen you in times of need. There is so much happening in the spiritual world around you. My angels are protecting you from unseen danger. Draw your strength from Me and continue moving in the direction I am leading you in. You will have peace and rest in the arms of your Savior.

> "Because he has set his love upon Me, therefore I will deliver him; I will set him on high because he has known My name. He shall call upon Me, and I will answer him; I *will be* with him in trouble; I will deliver him and honor him." (Psalm 91:14–15)
>
> For He shall give His angels charge over you, To keep you in all your ways. (Psalm 91:11)

67

SHINE MY LIGHT

KEEP MY COMMANDMENTS. LISTEN AND obey My voice. It will be health and healing to your bones. Nothing will touch you that I do not allow. My light within you will not be quenched. It will shine as brightly as the noon sun. The rays of light will reach out to those around you, gently drawing others to Me. Continue loving others and shining My light. It will have far-reaching effects in this world and the world to come.

> Do not be wise in your own eyes; Fear the Lord and depart from evil. It will be health to your flesh, And strength to your bones. (Proverbs 3:7–8)

> A new commandment I give to you, that you love one another; as I have loved you, that you also love one another. (John 13:34)

SOW GOOD SEEDS

*T*HE WAY YOU LIVE YOUR life and the decisions you make will determine what you will reap. There is a principle I have set in motion to be lived out. If you do good, you will reap back this good more than you have sowed, in due time. If you sow to the flesh and do evil, you will reap this back also. Rest assured, there will be a harvest to come from the seeds you have sown. Sow good seeds and walk in the Spirit.

> Do not be deceived, God is not mocked; for whatsoever a man sows, that he will also reap. For he who sows to his flesh will of the flesh reap corruption, but he who sows to the Spirit will of the Spirit reap everlasting life. (Galatians 6:7–8)
>
> If we live by the Spirit, let us also walk in the Spirit. (Galatians 5:25)

SPEAK THE TRUTHS OF MY WORD

*S*PEAK THE TRUTHS OF MY Word. Live them out in your daily life. Be kind to all. Show mercy and grace with compassion and understanding. Open your heart to be a good listener. Think before you speak. Let the language of your heart and mind be acceptable in My sight. How you live your life matters to Me. I want to meet all of your needs. I will empower you to live a Christlike life.

> Let us therefore come boldly to the throne of grace, that we may obtain mercy and find grace to help in time of need. (Hebrews 4:16)

> Let the words of my mouth and the meditation of my heart Be acceptable in Your sight, O Lord, my strength and my Redeemer. (Psalm 19:14)

70

SPIRITUAL FOOD

*W*SDOM IS GIVEN TO THOSE who open My Word and digest its content. It is spiritual food that never loses its flavor. It gives satisfaction to those who savor it in their heart and mind. You will be strengthened and energized by partaking of its content. It is needed for sustenance to live the Christian life. Listen carefully to Me and eat what is good.

> All ate the same spiritual food, and all drank the same spiritual drink. For they drank of that spiritual Rock that followed them, and that Rock was Christ. (1 Corinthians 10:3–4)

> Why do you spend money for *what* is not bread, And your wages for *what* does not satisfy? Listen carefully to Me, and eat *what* is good, And let your soul delight itself in abundance. (Isaiah 55:2)

71

THE ABUNDANT LIFE

I AM THE WAY, THE TRUTH, and the life. No one comes to the Father except through Me. I have made a way for all who accept Me and the sacrifice I have made for them. Repent of your sins and accept Me as Lord and Savior of your life. I will come into your heart and help you live the abundant life. A life dedicated to Me will have favor and blessings in abundance. Don't look back; look forward to all that I have waiting for you.

> Jesus said to him, "I am the way, the truth, and the life, No one comes to the Father except through Me." (John 14:6)

> The Lord is not slack concerning His promise, as some count slackness, but is longsuffering toward us, not willing that any should perish but that all should come to repentance. (2 Peter 3:9)

THE ACTION OF SURRENDER

My PEOPLE WHO ARE CALLED by My name need to humble themselves and pray. I will hear from heaven and answer their prayers. Your earnest voices, as well as your thoughts, are heard. I am always ready and open to having a conversation with you. I am your protector and defender, for I never slumber or sleep. Align your will to My will, for this action of surrender will bring contentment and peace to your soul. Surrender is the very action necessary to enjoy the amazing plan I have in store for your life. You will experience small glimpses of heaven by living a life totally surrendered to Me.

> "If My people who are called by My name will humble themselves, and pray and seek My face, and turn from their wicked ways, then I will hear from heaven and will forgive their sin and heal their land." (2 Chronicles 7:14)

> "I have been crucified with Christ; it is no longer I who live, but Christ lives in me; and the *life* which I now live in the flesh I live by faith in the Son of God who loved me and gave Himself for me." (Galatians 2:20)

THE BIBLE GIVES US INSTRUCTION

*G*IVING OUT THE GOSPEL IS so important. It is profound wisdom for all. It is God breathed. It encourages and gives hope. The Bible gives instruction on how to live your life. It is full of prophecy of things to come and already fulfilled prophecy. Learn from My Word what is required of you—to do justly, to love mercy, and to walk humbly with your God.

> All Scripture *is* given by inspiration of God, and *is* profitable for doctrine, for reproof, for correction, for instruction in righteousness, that the man of God may be complete, thoroughly equipped for every good work. (2 Timothy 3:16–17)

> He has shown you, O man what *is* good; And what does the Lord require of you But to do justly, To love *mercy*, And to walk humbly with your God? (Micah 6:8)

74

THE HOPE OF GLORY

I AM CHRIST IN YOU, THE hope of glory. This has been revealed to My saints. We are united together as one body. My goal is that I may dwell in your heart through faith and that you are rooted and grounded in My love. My will is carried out through you as you live out these virtues. Be fruitful in every good work, increasing in the knowledge of God.

> The mystery which has been hidden from ages and from generations, but now has been revealed to His saints. To them God willed to make known what are the riches of the glory of the mystery among the Gentiles: which is Christ in you, the hope of glory. (Colossians 1:26–27)
>
> That Christ may dwell in your hearts through faith; that you, being rooted and grounded in love. (Ephesians 3:17)

75

THE LIGHTED PATHWAY

*W*ALK ALONG THE PATH I have prepared for you. There may be some rocks along the way, but I will help you get over and around them. The path of life I have prepared is not always easy, but I have given you a Helper. Following My path will bless you with joy and peace. The Helper will light up the way in which you should go. Follow your lighted pathway. There is great reward at the end of this road. Have complete trust as you journey down the road that is lit for you to follow.

> "You shall walk in all the ways which the Lord your God has commanded you, that you may live and *that it may be* well with you, and *that* you may prolong *your* days in the land which you shall possess." (Deuteronomy 5:33)

> "I have heard of you, that the Spirit of God is in you, and that light and understanding and excellent wisdom are found in you." (Daniel 5:14)

THE POWER OF THE TONGUE

THE TONGUE IS A TINY member but with so much power. Who can tame the tongue? Your thoughts affect the power of the tongue. Saturate yourself in My Word so your thought pattern will reflect wisdom flowing from your tongue. Words lift up, and words tear down. Make sure your words are lifting up and encouraging others. This will reflect Me in your life.

> Out of the same mouth proceed blessing and cursing. My brethren, these things ought not to be so. (James 3:10)

> Let no corrupt word proceed out of your mouth, but what is good for necessary edification, that it may impart grace to the hearers. (Ephesians 4:29)

77

THE RIGHTEOUS WILL FLOURISH

I AM YOUR STRONG REFUGE, WHICH you may resort to continually. Trouble will come, but you will be sheltered and safe in My arms. I will give you the strength to overcome any obstacle you face. I am your rock and your fortress. I will cause the righteous to flourish like a palm tree. Your beauty will grow as you continue to grow in your relationship with Me.

> Be my strong refuge, To which I may resort continually; You have given the commandment to save me, For You *are* my rock and my fortress. (Psalm 71:3)

> The righteous shall flourish like a palm tree, He shall grow like a cedar in Lebanon. Those who are planted in the house of the Lord Shall flourish in the courts of our God. (Psalm 92:12–13)

THE SPIRIT OF TRUTH

*W*HEN YOU BECOME MY CHILD, you have the Spirit of truth living in you. My Spirit assures you of the truths of My Word and reveals to you the truth of who I am. You see God more clearly by the Spirit of truth who lives within you. He empowers you to believe and know the great love God has for you. You have the power to overcome because of My Spirit who lives in you. He is always available and willing to teach you all things.

> "And I will pray the Father, and He will give you another Helper, that He may abide with you forever—" the Spirit of truth, whom the world cannot receive, because it neither sees Him nor knows Him; but you know Him, for He dwells with you and will be in you. (John 14:16–17)

> And we have known and believed the love that God has for us. God is love, and he who abides in love abides in God, and God in him. (1 John 4:16)

79

THE VICTORIOUS LIFE

*B*E CALM AND TRUST ME for a blessed day, regardless of your situation. I am here to help you have victory in all circumstances. Trusting Me is key to a victorious life. When trials of life come, I am with you. Storms of life come and go, but I continue to stand with you. Trust Me to bring you through the storms of life raging around you. I am your defender; you shall not be moved.

> He only *is* my rock and my salvation; *He is* my defense; I shall not be moved. (Psalm 62:6)

> "For the Lord your God is He who goes with you, to fight for you against your enemies, to save you." (Deuteronomy 20:4)

THE WIND AND THE SPIRIT

THE HOLY SPIRIT HAS BEEN compared to the wind. You can't really see it, but you can feel it. You can see the evidence of the wind. It varies in strength and power of what it can do. The more you expose yourself, the stronger it becomes. It can change its course or become very still so that it is not felt at all. The wind can push you along when at your back, helping you to get to your destination sooner. There is an ease and a flow when you are going in the same direction. It can be very powerful.

> "The wind blows where it wishes, and you hear the sound of it, but cannot tell where it comes from and where it goes. So is everyone who is born of the Spirit." (John 3:8)

> For what man knows the things of a man except the spirit of the man which is in him? Even so no one know the things of God except the Spirit of God. (1 Corinthians 2:11)

81

TIME IS A PERFECT GIFT

*G*IVING OF YOUR TIME IS a perfect gift—wrapped in love, care, and compassion for others. Use your time wisely. Everything needs to be in balance. Spend time with Me daily, speaking and listening. Spend time caring for the needs of others in words and deeds. You are planting seeds of faith that will grow unto Me. What you do for the least of these, you have done for Me.

> I planted, Apollos watered, but God gave the increase. So neither he who plants is anything, nor he who waters, but God who gives the increase. Now he who plants and he who waters are one, and each one will receive his own reward according to his own labor. (1 Corinthians 3:6–8)

> "And the king will answer and say to them, 'Assuredly, I say to you, inasmuch as you did *it* to one of the least of these My brethren, you did *it* to Me.'" (Matthew 25:40)

82

TRUST ME

*W*ORSHIP IS A FORM OF surrender to Me. Surrender your will to Me. Worship Me in spirit and in truth, for I know your thoughts before you speak them. Clear your thoughts so I can speak to you. Believe Me and trust Me with your life. A joyful heart will rest peacefully. I am your joy. Do not look elsewhere for it. I am the only one who can satisfy the longing of your soul.

> "God is Spirit, and those who worship Him must worship in spirit and truth." (John 4:24)

> These things I have spoken to you, that My joy may remain in you, and that your joy may be full. (John 15:11)

83

UNENDING LOVE

LOVE UNENDING IS MY GIFT. A complete love. A love that sees past any faults. A love that is transparent, seen by all who dare to trust Me, all who hope in Me. An everlasting love that nurtures and cares for you. It is indescribable. Your mind cannot comprehend the capacity of My love for you.

> For I am persuaded that neither death nor life, nor angels nor principalities nor powers, nor things present nor things to come, nor height nor depth, nor any other created thing, shall be able to separate us from the love of God which is in Christ Jesus our Lord. (Romans 8:38–39)

> And now abide faith, hope, love, these three; but the greatest of these is love. (1 Corinthians 13:13)

WALK THROUGH OPEN DOORS

I WILL OPEN DOORS FOR YOU to get My will accomplished in your life. Walk through those open doors and follow My leading. Together we can accomplish mighty and great things for God, our heavenly Father. Be ready to speak the words of wisdom I impart to you. Be ready to give an answer to those who ask for the reason of hope and contentment within you.

> Furthermore, when I came to Troas to *preach* Christ's gospel, and a door was opened to me by the Lord. (2 Corinthians 2:12)

> But sanctify the Lord God in your hearts, and always *be* ready to *give* a defense to everyone who asks you as reason for the hope that is in you, with meekness and fear. (1 Peter 3:15)

85

WALK WORTHY OF THE CALLING

WALK WORTHY OF THE CALLING for which you've been called. Be My mouthpiece. Speak My words of truth in love, with humility and gentleness. Listen to Me and move forward in obedience. Joining Me will give you a deep satisfaction of accomplishment in your life. Together we will soar on the wings like eagles. We will run and not grow weary. We are partners in this journey of life everlasting.

> I, therefore, the prisoner of the Lord, beseech you to walk worthy of the calling with which you were called, with all lowliness and gentleness, with longsuffering, bearing with one another in love. (Ephesians 4:1–2)

> But those who wait on the Lord Shall renew *their* strength; They shall mount up with wings like eagles, They shall run and not be weary, They shall walk and not faint. (Isaiah 40:31)

WHERE IS YOUR TREASURE?

I HAVE GIVEN YOU MANY PRECIOUS promises for setting your love upon Me. I will be with you when trouble comes. When you call upon My name, I will answer you. I will deliver you and honor you. What do you treasure most in your life? That is where your heart will be. Guard your heart because everything you do flows from it. Your flesh and your heart may fail, but God is the strength of your heart and your portion forever. Let your heart follow after Me, your treasure.

> "Because he has set his love upon Me, therefore I will deliver him; I will set him on high, because he has known My name." (Psalm 91:14)

> "For where your treasure is, there your heart will be also." (Matthew 6:21)

87

WISDOM CRIES OUT

*W*ISDOM CRIES OUT TO YOU, and those who diligently seek Me will find Me, for wisdom is greater than rubies. Wisdom is the greatest jewel you can possess. Wisdom will guide you into all truth. Those who are wise will find favor from the Lord. Great understanding will accompany you when you cry out for wisdom. The fear of the Lord is the beginning of wisdom. The fruit of wisdom is better than fine gold.

> Does not wisdom cry out, And understanding lift up her voice? (Proverbs 8:1)

> The fear of the Lord is the beginning of wisdom, And the knowledge of the Holy One is understanding. (Proverbs 9:10)

WORDS ARE POWERFUL

*W*ORDS ARE POWERFUL. SPEAK LIFE with your words—words that lift up, words that comfort, and words that bring peace to the soul. Encouragement is a precious gift of words to help someone move forward in whatever task they need to accomplish, with positive energy and excitement toward their goal. Words can also tear down and discourage. Be careful to choose your words wisely.

> Death and life *are* in the power of the tongue, and those who love it will eat its fruit. (Proverbs 18:21)

> The hypocrite with *his* mouth destroys his neighbor, but through knowledge the righteous will be delivered. (Proverbs 11:9)

WORDS OF WISDOM

*S*PEAK WORDS OF WISDOM. A still tongue can be evidence of wisdom. Silence at times can be golden. Words have so much more meaning when spoken with a clean heart. Stay humble and true to Me. Keep Me in your thoughts. Lift your voice to heaven and ask for My wisdom. It will give health and healing to your bones. Peace will abound.

> In the multitude of words sin is not lacking, But he who restrains his lips *is* wise. (Proverbs 10:19)

> If any of you lacks wisdom, let him ask of God, who gives to all liberally and without *reproach*, and it will be given to him. (James 1:5)

WORLDLY DISTRACTIONS

*D*ISTRACTIONS ARE ONE OF SATAN'S tools to draw your focus away from Me. Make an effort to spend time with Me, away from phones, texts, computers, calls, and other distractions. This age of constant interruptions from phones ringing and dinging will keep you from spending quality time with Me. You need quiet, uninterrupted time to hear My voice and digest the Word of God. Pick a time of quiet to focus on our relationship. It is necessary for growth and contentment.

> Do not love the world or the things in the world. If anyone loves the world, the love of the Father is not him in. (1 John 2:15)

> If then you were raised with Christ, seek those things which are above, where Christ is sitting, at the right hand of God.

> Set your mind on things above, not on things on the earth. (Colossians 3:1–2)

91

YOU ARE GOD'S TEMPLE

*B*URST FORTH WITH SINGING TO your heavenly Father who created the heavens and the earth. Worship Him in the sanctuary of your heart. You are God's temple, and His Spirit dwells within you. Cherish the fact that the Holy Spirit lives within you, My child, giving you all you need to live the Christian life. Take comfort in the fact that wisdom, knowledge, and understanding are imparted to you by Him. He will teach you all things.

> Do you not know that you are the temple of God and that the Spirit of God dwells in you? (1 Corinthians 3:16)

> "The Spirit of truth, whom the world cannot receive, because it neither sees Him nor knows Him; but you know Him, for He dwells with you and will be in you." (John 14:17)

92

YOU ARE IN A BATTLE

*C*AST YOUR CARES UPON ME. I am able to turn your fears and doubts into blessings. Be aware of the source of the thoughts that enter your mind. Remember you are in a battle between good and evil. Satan will try to penetrate your mind with lies. Resist the devil, and he will flee. Draw close to me so you will recognize his lies. Ask for My help, and I will show you truth. You will be more than a conqueror through Me, who loves you more than you could imagine.

> Casting all your *care* upon Him, for He cares for you. (1 Peter 5:7)

> Therefore submit to God. Resist the devil and he will flee from you. (James 4:7)

93

YOU ARE NOT ALONE

Fix YOUR EYES UPON ME. Look up and remember I am with you wherever you go. You are not alone. Rejoice in the fact that I am holding your right hand. I have given angels charge over you. Be at peace in the midst of any storm you encounter. I will give you all that you need to navigate through this life. Enjoy the journey. Open yourself up to change. Nothing ever stays the same. Only My love for you is never changing. It is steady and sure.

> For He shall give His angels charge over you, to keep you in all your ways. (Psalm 91:11)
>
> For I, the Lord your God, will hold your right hand, Saying to you, "Fear not, I will help you." (Isaiah 41:13)

94

YOU ARE PRECIOUS TO ME

$\mathcal{S}$URELY GOODNESS AND MERCY WILL follow you all the days of your life, and you will dwell in the house of the Lord forever. My promises are true. Be not dismayed, for I am your God, the lifter of your head. I will be with you until the end of the age. You are very precious to Me. Therefore, you shall lay up these words of mine in your heart and soul.

> Surely goodness and mercy shall follow me All the days of my life; and I will dwell in the house of the Lord Forever. (Psalm 23:6)

> "Therefore you shall lay up these words of mine in your heart and in your soul, and bind them as a sign on your hand, and they shall be as frontlets between your eyes." (Deuteronomy 11:18)

YOUR LIFE IS A BOOK

I AM YOUR HIDING PLACE. YOU may rest under the shadow of My wings. You are safe and secure as you walk by faith through the pages of your life. Your life is a book that others read as you choose what actions will be shown daily. Will your book be about love, joy, kindness, gentleness, and peace? Let these attributes leap off the pages of your story, written for others to see.

> You *are* my hiding place and my shield; I hope in your word. (Psalm 119:114)

> Being confident of this very thing, that He who has begun a good work in you will complete it until the day of Jesus Christ. (Philippians 1:6)

96

YOUR LIFE JOURNEY

*T*HE SPIRITUALLY MINDED WILL HAVE life and peace. You need peace to enjoy life. I so want you to enjoy this journey called life. Oh, how you enjoy life when you serve others. You will get a euphoric feeling when you bless others in this life. It is a gift from me when you choose to bless those in need. Your hands and feet in motion, extending My love to others, makes me feel a joy unspeakable. I enjoy walking beside you in your life journey.

> For to be carnally minded is death, but to be spiritually minded is life and peace. (Romans 8:6)
>
> But do not forget to do good and to share, for with such sacrifices God is well pleased. (Hebrews 13:16)

97

YOUR LIFE STORY

My PROTECTION AND COMFORT ARE with you every day. I give the angels the ability to watch over you. You are writing a story with your life. Others read your story by watching your life. Think about what you want them to see. Ask for My help daily so that your life story will glorify Me. We are partners in this life. I want your life story to reap many benefits, such as joy, peace, favor, and blessings. My love is ever present with you. Put your faith and trust in Me, for I will help you to live a victorious life.

> "For it is written: 'He shall give His angels charge over you, To keep you,' and, 'In their hands they shall bear you up, Lest you dash your foot against a stone.'" (Luke 4:10–11)

> The Lord shall preserve you from all evil; He shall preserve your soul. The Lord shall preserve your going out and your coming in, From this time forth, and even forevermore. (Psalm 121:7–8)

YOUR SINS HAVE BEEN FORGIVEN

*F*ORGIVE AS YOU HAVE BEEN forgiven. Rejoice in the fact that your sins have been forgiven. Rest in the peace of My presence. I watch over you and guard you from the enemy. Resist the devil, and he will flee from you. Cast your cares upon Me. I am more than able to carry them for you. Seek Me, and you will find Me. I am so much closer than you think. I am watching over you. Be at peace.

> Bearing with one another, and *forgiving* one another, if anyone has a complaint against another; even as Christ forgave you, so you also *must do*. (Colossians 3:13)

> Therefore submit to God. Resist the devil and he will flee from you. (James 4:7)

99

YOUR THOUGHT PATTERN

*E*XCHANGE YOUR THOUGHT PATTERN FOR Mine. Actions follow your thought pattern. Make sure your thoughts are aligned with My teaching. You tend to falter when worldly thoughts influence your life. Recognize this tendency and refocus your thoughts back on Me and My teaching. Remember to ask for My wisdom so that your path in life will be easier. Worldly wisdom is not your friend. I am your friend who will stick closer than a brother.

> That you put off, concerning your former conduct, the old man which grows corrupt according to the deceitful lusts, and be renewed in the spirit of your mind. (Ephesians 4:22–23)

> A man *who has* friends must himself be friendly, But there is a friend who sticks closer than a brother. (Proverbs 18:2)

YOUR WORDS MATTER

May YOUR SPEECH BE WITH honesty and clarity of thought. Your words matter. You are my ambassadors in this world. Represent Me well. Let your actions show humility and mercy to all. Do not be wise in your own eyes but seek My wisdom from above. I will help you walk in My ways and, in essence, show a Christlike manner to a hurting world. Show My love to all who cross your path.

> Let no corrupt word proceed out of your mouth, but what is good for necessary edification, that it may impart grace to the hearers. (Ephesians 4:29)

> Be of the same mind toward one another. Do not set your mind on high things, but associate with the humble. Do not be wise in your own opinion. (Romans 12:16)